D0118794

GRIZZLY BEAR

Joseph Stanley

New York

Published in 2016 by The Rosen Publishing Group, Inc.
29 East 21st Street, New York, NY 10010

First Edition

Editor: Katie Kawa
Book Design: Reann Nye

Photo Credits: Cover (background) Jim David/Shutterstock.com; cover (grizzly bear), p. 1 Jody Dingle/Shutterstock.com; p. 4 neelsky/Shutterstock.com; p. 5 BGSmith/Shutterstock.com; pp. 6, 11 Andrea Izzotti/Shutterstock.com; p. 7 Volodymyr Burdiak/Shutterstock.com; pp. 8–9 AndreAnita/Shutterstock.com; p. 9 (map) boreala/Shutterstock.com p. 10 Stephen J Krasemann/All Canada Photos/Getty Images; pp. 12, 19 David Rasmus/Shutterstock.com; p. 13 DPS/Shutterstock.com; pp. 14, 15 (grasses) AndreAnita/Shutterstock.com; p. 15 (fruits) FotograFFF/Shutterstock.coml; p. 15 (fish) bierchen/Shutterstock.com; pp. 15 (elk), 21 Tom Reichner/Shutterstock.com; p. 15 (background) Aleksandar Mijatovic/Shutterstock.com; p. 16 Eugene Gurkov/Shutterstock.com; p. 17 Galyna Andrushko/Shutterstock.com; p. 18 Scott E Read/Shutterstock.com; p. 20 Andrew Swaner/Shutterstock.com; p. 22 outdoorsman/Shutterstock.com.

Cataloging-in-Publication Data

Stanley, Joseph.
Grizzly bear / by Joseph Stanley.
p. cm. — (North America's biggest beasts)
Includes index.
ISBN 978-1-5081-4294-2 (pbk.)
ISBN 978-1-5081-4295-9 (6-pack)
ISBN 978-1-5081-4299-7 (library binding)
1. Grizzly bear — Juvenile literature. I. Stanley, Joseph. II. Title.
QL737.C27 S73 2016
599.784—d23

Manufactured in the United States of America

CPSIA Compliance Information: Batch #BW16PK: For Further Information contact Rosen Publishing, New York, New York at 1-800-237-9932

CONTENTS

Big Brown Bears

Brown bears are some of the largest **mammals** in North America! There are different kinds of brown bears that call this **continent** home. One of these is the grizzly bear. Grizzly bears got their name from the silver or white tips of their fur, because "grizzled" means **streaked** with gray.

How big are these bears? An adult male grizzly bear can weigh over 800 pounds (363 kg). If it stands on its hind, or back, legs, it can rise to a height of 8 feet (2.4 m).

Kodiak bear

THE BIG IDEA

The largest brown bear in North America is the Kodiak bear, which is only found on certain islands in Alaska. Kodiak bears can weigh up to 1,720 pounds (780 kg)!

Grizzly bears and Kodiak bears use their large size to hunt other animals.

A Closer Look

Grizzly bears are known for their grizzled fur. Their fur is mainly brown and can be many shades—from dark brown to light tan. Grizzly bears have claws on their feet. The claws on their front feet are very long. These claws help them dig for food and create dens, or places to live in the winter. Grizzly bears also use their claws to mark the trees around the area where they live.

Grizzly bears also have a large shoulder hump made of **muscle**. This hump gives them extra strength when they're digging.

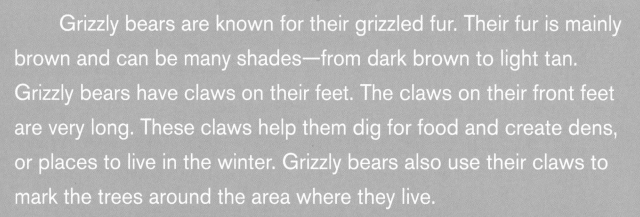

THE BIG IDEA

If you see scratches on trees or trees missing bark, a grizzly bear might be in the area.

shoulder hump

Grizzly bears also use their shoulder hump to move logs and rocks when looking for food.

A Shrinking Habitat

Grizzly bears used to live throughout the western part of North America. They even lived on the Great Plains! However, their **range** shrank as people settled in the West and began hunting them. Today, grizzly bears live mainly in Canada and Alaska. A small number live in other parts of the United States, such as Yellowstone National Park, which is located mainly in Wyoming.

Grizzly bears live in many different kinds of **habitats**. They can be found in forests, meadows, and **prairies**.

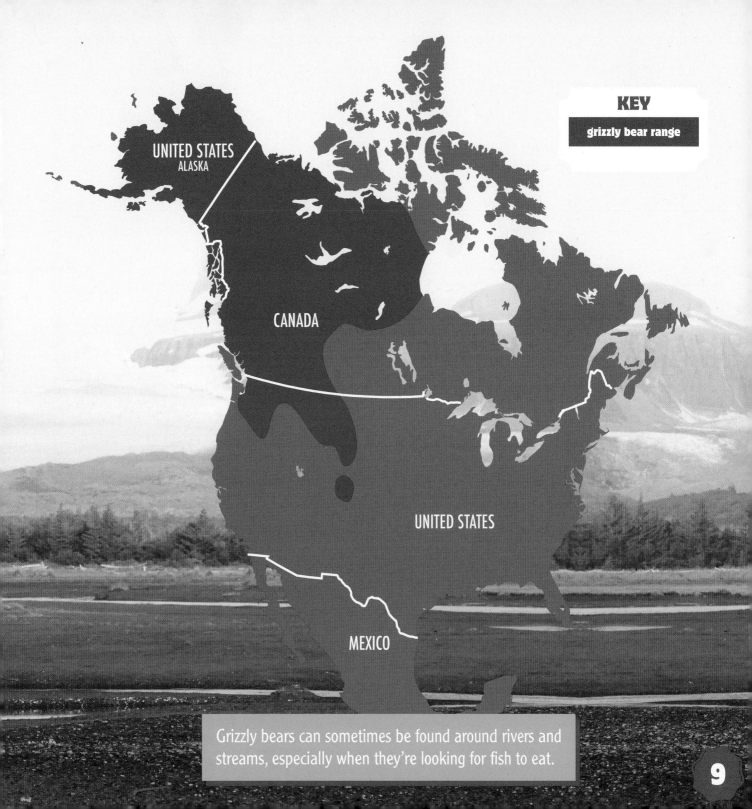

KEY

grizzly bear range

UNITED STATES
ALASKA

CANADA

UNITED STATES

MEXICO

Grizzly bears can sometimes be found around rivers and streams, especially when they're looking for fish to eat.

Deep Sleep

Grizzly bears live in some of the coldest places in North America. This makes it hard for them to find food in the winter. Instead of staying outside in the cold, many grizzly bears build dens to stay in throughout the winter months.

In late summer and fall, grizzly bears build up a lot of fat in their body. They live off this supply of fat while in a period of deep sleep called torpor. Their body **temperature** goes down, and their heart rate slows.

grizzly bear den

THE BIG IDEA

Grizzly bears don't go into a state of true **hibernation** in the winter. They can still be woken up, which couldn't happen if they were truly hibernating.

Grizzly bears use their den to stay safe and warm as they sleep through the winter.

Cute Cubs

Dens aren't just places where grizzly bears sleep in the winter. They're also where baby grizzly bears, which are called cubs, are born. Mother grizzly bears give birth to their cubs during the winter. They often have two cubs at once.

Cubs stay with their mother for at least two years. She feeds them, and she also helps them learn to find food for themselves. Cubs may stay with their mother longer than two years if they live in places without much food.

THE BIG IDEA

Male grizzly bears don't play a part in raising cubs. In fact, grizzly bears are generally solitary animals, except for mothers and cubs. Solitary animals live alone rather than as part of a group.

Mother grizzly bears are very **protective** of their cubs.

Hungry Omnivores

Grizzly bears need to eat a lot of food because they're such large mammals. They're omnivores, which means they eat both plants and animals. While grizzly bears are predators, much of the food they eat consists of plants, such as berries, leaves, and roots.

However, grizzly bears also love to eat meat. They hunt small mammals, such as squirrels, as well as larger mammals, such as moose and deer. Grizzly bears often hunt the babies of these larger mammals. They eat bugs, too.

THE BIG IDEA

Grizzly bears sometimes eat carrion, which is another name for animals that are already dead.

WHAT DO GRIZZLY BEARS EAT?

nuts	mice
fruits	fish
carrion	sheep
grasses	elk
moth larvae (baby moths)	mountain goats

These are just some of the foods grizzly bears have been known to eat.

From Hunters to Hunted

Grizzly bears are great hunters because of their size and strength. These things also help them avoid being another animal's meal! Grizzly bears don't have many known predators. Cubs are most in danger of being eaten by other animals. They're sometimes hunted by other bears, mountain lions, or wolf packs. This doesn't happen often, though.

People are a grizzly bear's biggest enemy. They've been hunting these bears for hundreds of years. Hunters in Canada and Alaska still kill grizzly bears for sport.

THE BIG IDEA

Grizzly bears are big, but they're also fast. They can run at speeds of up to 30 miles (48 km) per hour.

A grizzly bear's size often **protects** it from other animals, but a big body is no match for a hunter with a gun!

17

Grizzly Bears and People

Farmers don't like grizzly bears because bears have been known to eat livestock, such as cattle and sheep. However, farmers aren't the only people who are afraid of grizzly bears. These bears are often thought of as **dangerous** animals.

Although grizzly bears do attack people, that doesn't happen very often. Grizzly bears generally avoid contact with people. If a grizzly bear does attack a person, it's often because the bear was startled. Mother grizzly bears have also been known to attack if they feel their cubs are in danger.

THE BIG IDEA

If you see a bear, stay far away from it. If a bear gets close to you, talk to it in a calm voice. Don't run, but slowly back away.

People think of grizzly bears as very scary animals. However, these bears want to stay away from people whenever they can.

Protecting Grizzly Bears

While hunting grizzly bears is still allowed in Alaska and Canada, these animals are protected in the rest of the United States. South of Canada, grizzly bears are considered endangered, or at risk of dying out. There are only about 1,000 grizzly bears alive in the United States outside of Alaska.

People are working to protect grizzly bears by making safe places for them to live. These places include national parks, such as Yellowstone National Park. Protecting grizzly bears' natural habitats in Canada and Alaska is also very important.

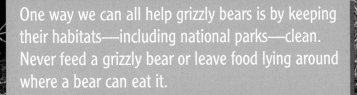

One way we can all help grizzly bears is by keeping their habitats—including national parks—clean. Never feed a grizzly bear or leave food lying around where a bear can eat it.

21

Powerful Predators

Another way people are working to protect grizzly bears is by educating others about these animals. As people learn more about these big bears, they discover grizzly bears generally don't want to harm people. However, grizzly bears are still dangerous predators and should be treated as such.

Grizzly bears are amazing animals, but it's best to admire them from far away. It's safer for both you and the bears. Their huge size and strong body make them one of the most powerful predators in North America!

Glossary

continent: One of the seven great masses of land on Earth.

dangerous: Not safe.

habitat: The natural home for plants, animals, and other living things.

hibernation: The act of sleeping or resting all winter without waking up.

mammal: Any warm-blooded animal whose babies drink milk and whose body is covered with hair or fur.

muscle: A part of the body that produces motion.

prairie: A large, mostly flat type of land in North America that has few trees and is covered in grasses.

protect: To keep safe.

protective: Showing a strong wish to keep someone or something safe from harm.

range: The open area of land over which animals move and feed.

streaked: Marked with stripes.

temperature: How hot or cold something is.

Index

A
Alaska, 4, 8, 9, 16, 20

C
Canada, 8, 9, 16, 20
carrion, 14, 15
cubs, 12, 13, 16, 18

D
danger, 16, 18, 22
dens, 6, 10, 11, 12

F
food, 6, 10, 12, 14, 15, 21
fur, 4, 6

G
Great Plains, 8

H
habitats, 8, 20, 21
hibernation, 10
hunt, 5, 8, 14, 16, 17, 20

K
Kodiak bears, 4, 5

M
mammals, 4, 14

O
omnivores, 14

R
range, 8

T
torpor, 10

W
Wyoming, 8

Y
Yellowstone National Park, 8, 20

Websites

Due to the changing nature of Internet links, PowerKids Press has developed an online list of websites related to the subject of this book. This site is updated regularly. Please use this link to access the list: www.powerkidslinks.com/nabb/grzz